FAITH, COURAGE AND PERSEVERANCE

A STUDY IN EZRA

BIBLE STUDIES TO IMPACT THE LIVES OF ORDINARY PEOPLE

The Word Worldwide

CHRISTIAN FOCUS

For details of our titles visit us on our website
www.christianfocus.com

ISBN 1-85792-949-7

Copyright © WEC International

Published in 2004 by
Christian Focus Publications, Geanies House,
Fearn, Ross-shire, IV20 ITW, Scotland
and
WEC International, Bulstrode, Oxford Road,
Gerrards Cross, Bucks, SL9 8SZ

Cover design by Alister MacInnes

Printed and bound by J W Arrowsmith, Bristol

CONTENTS

QUESTIONS AND NOTES

ANSWER GUIDE

PREFACE
GEARED FOR GROWTH

**'Where there's LIFE there's GROWTH:
Where there's GROWTH there's LIFE.'**

WHY GROW a study group?

Because as we study the Bible and share together we can

- learn to combat loneliness, depression, staleness, frustration, and other problems
- get to understand and love each other
- become responsive to the Holy Spirit's dealing and obedient to God's Word

and that's GROWTH.

How do you GROW a study group?

- Just start by asking a friend to join you and then aim at expanding your group.
- Study the set portions daily (they are brief and easy: no catches).
- Meet once a week to discuss what you find.
- Befriend others, both Christians and non Christians, and work away together

see how it GROWS!

WHEN you GROW ...

This will happen at school, at home, at work, at play, in your youth group, your student fellowship, women's meetings, mid-week meetings, churches and communities,

you'll be REACHING THROUGH TEACHING

INTRODUCTORY STUDY

How much do you know about the ancient history of the Jewish nation?
    Who was its founder? (Gen. 12:1-3)
    Which land did God give His people? (Gen. 13:12, 14-17)
    Several generations later, why did they move to Egypt? (Gen. 45:9-11)
    What happened to the nation in Egypt? (Exod. 1:8-14)
    Who did God use to bring His people out of Egypt? (Exod. 3:10-12)
    Who led the people into the land of Canaan? (Josh. 1:1-5)
    Who established Jerusalem as a royal city? (2 Sam. 5:6-10)
    Who built the first Temple? (2 Chron. 3:1)

About 350 years later (587 BC):
    What happened to the Temple? (2 Kgs. 25:8-15)
    What happened to the Jewish people? (2 Chron. 36:18-20)
    How did the people feel? (Ps. 137)

It was during the time of the exile in Babylon that the prophet Jeremiah proclaimed a message of hope from God. Read it in Jeremiah 29:10-14.
    What was God's promise to His people?
    An even more amazing prophecy came from Isaiah. Before the Jews had ever heard of anyone called Cyrus, God sent this message: Isaiah 44:28; 45:1-3, 13.
    Can you imagine the hope that was kindled in the hearts of God's people? And when the Persians under King Cyrus conquered Babylon around 538 BC, don't you think there would have been a buzz of excitement in every Jewish home?
    Only months later came the proclamation from the king. Look it up – Ezra has recorded it right at the beginning of his book.

* * *

You might like to pause here to praise the mighty God that we too serve. Praise Him in prayer, and perhaps you could sing a song like:

      Great is the Lord (Scripture in Song 70)
      Our Lord is Wonderful (Scripture in Song 324)
  or To God be the Glory.
    (**Leaders**, you might bring a cassette of praise songs.)

* * *

Although the book is named EZRA after its author, he is not the main character of the book, appearing only in the last four chapters. The earlier heroes are ZERUBBABEL, the governor of princely descent, and JOSHUA the High Priest. The book covers a period of eighty years, from the first year of Cyrus to the eighth year of Artaxerxes, King of Persia.

You will see in Ezra chapter 2 the list of people who returned to Jerusalem with Zerubbabel and Joshua. How many people came (v. 64)? However, there were many more Jews in exile who preferred to remain in the comparative luxury of Babylon. Those who chose to return needed:

FAITH
    COURAGE
        and PERSEVERANCE.

FAITH, COURAGE and PERSEVERANCE. Look out for these 3 words as we study.

Only a few courageous people under the leadership of Zerubbabel and Joshua elected to return to their own land to rebuild their temple and city. What a temptation it is to choose the easy way! Yet what joy to those men and women of faith, courage and perseverance who faced the trials and difficulties that lay ahead, and saw the temple, emblem of their God among them, raised up in their midst.

Later, Ezra, scribe and teacher of the law, with a further company of restored captives, came to join them. And around the same time the godly Nehemiah came to rebuild the walls that were still lying in ruins.

The books of the Bible that relate to this period of history are Ezra, Nehemiah, Esther, Daniel, Zechariah and Haggai. The events relating to the return of the exiles to Jerusalem and of the rebuilding, not only of the temple, but of their nation, are discussed in the following pages. There is much to learn that will inspire us to accept God's challenges, much to encourage us in our times of adversity, and to assure us that as we obey and trust God, He will give us the joy of victory over our adversary Satan.

STUDY 1

THE DECREE OF KING CYRUS

QUESTIONS

DAY 1 *Jeremiah 25:11, 12; John 14:3; 1 Thessalonians 4:16-18; 2 Peter 1:20, 21.*
a) God caused Jeremiah's prophecies to be literally fulfilled. What Bible prophecies are yet to be fulfilled?

b) And how can we be sure that they will be fulfilled?

DAY 2 *Ezra 1:1; Isaiah 44:28; Proverbs 8:15; 1 Timothy 2:1, 2.*
The Lord moved the heart of Cyrus, as Isaiah had prophesied. Discuss whether God can move the hearts of people in authority to do His will today.

DAY 3 *Ezra 1:2-4.*
a) To what does King Cyrus attribute his military success?

b) How can God guide us to do His will today?

DAY 4 *Ezra 1:5; Acts 13:1-3; 15:22.*
a) Which particular people under King Cyrus organized the project?

b) Under King Jesus who should normally initiate new projects in the church's work?

QUESTIONS (contd.)

DAY 5 *Ezra 1:6.*
How do we see that their status as slaves had been modified under Persian rule?

DAY 6 *Ezra 1:6-11; I Timothy 5:17, 18; Philippians 4:16, 17.*
a) How were those who were not going, able to help the workers?

b) Whose responsibility is it to provide for our pastors, missionaries and other full time workers?

DAY 7 *Ezra 1:7.*
a) What can we learn here about the character of King Cyrus?

b) Should Christian workers be accountable in their use of funds?

NOTES

THE SOVEREIGNTY OF GOD

The hero of chapter one must surely be the Persian king Cyrus who had defeated the King of Babylon and succeeded to the throne of Babylon. Although God had chosen to use a cruel king Nebuchadnezzar to discipline the Jewish people for their rebellion, He had also decreed the fall of the mighty Babylon to a nation from the north, Persia (Jer. 50:3). Even King Cyrus's name is recorded as the deliverer of the Jewish nation long before his birth (Isa. 44:28). Proverbs 21:I tells us, 'The king's heart is a stream of water in the hand of the Lord; He turns it wherever He will.' How could we ever doubt the Word of God when we see how accurately it is fulfilled? And how could we ever doubt the sovereignty, wisdom and power of our God when we see how He is able to bring about His purposes in the earth?

CYRUS' DECREE

Although Cyrus must have been an idol worshipper, he acknowledges one God above all, who had enabled him to conquer all nations. He also claimed that this God had appointed him to build a temple in Jerusalem. Had he heard about the prophecy of Isaiah? We really don't know. But we do know that our sovereign God had spoken to him in some way, and put the desire into his heart to see the temple of Jerusalem rebuilt.

In the very first year of his reign he graciously made a decree that anyone who wished might go to Jerusalem to rebuild the temple that Nebuchadnezzar had destroyed. He also encouraged those who were not going to give generously towards the expenses involved.

Not all the people responded. Life was beginning to look good in Babylon under the Persian king, in contrast to the forced labour they had endured under the Babylonian kings. Why make the arduous desert journey to the land many of them had never seen, to face they did not know what? However, 'everyone whose heart God had moved' volunteered to make the long journey. Their neighbours, delighted to know the temple, the focal point of Judah's worship, was to be rebuilt, responded with gifts.

CYRUS'S FAITHFULNESS

And now we see a further admirable side of Cyrus's character. He brought out all the temple treasures that king Nebuchadnezzar had looted and stored in the temple of his god. In a systematic way an inventory was made, 5,400 articles in all, and committed to the hand of the faithful Zerubbabel (here called by his Persian name Sheshbazzar).

Zerubbabel was of royal blood, and was to be governor of the rebuilt province of Judah. And so the big venture is about to begin.

A verse to remember:
    'Your Word, O Lord, is eternal; it stands firm in the heavens. Your faithfulness continues throughout all generations' (Ps. II9:89, 90 niv).

STUDY 2

THE JOURNEY TO JERUSALEM

QUESTIONS

DAY 1 *Ezra 2:1.*
Look at a map of the Middle East and trace the journey the people would have taken from Babylon (near modern Bagdad) to Jerusalem. What type of country was it?

DAY 2 *Ezra 2:36-62; 1 Timothy 3:2-7.*
a) What groups of people are mentioned here?

b) Discuss what qualifications would equip a person to be recognized as a true Christian leader today.

DAY 3 *Ezra 2:63; Romans 12:1, 2; Psalm 119:105; Hebrews 13:7; Philippians 4:6, 7.*
URIM and THUMMIM were stones in the High Priest's breastplate. God used them in some mysterious way to show His will (See Num. 27:18-21, 1 Sam. 28:6). What are some of the ways God uses to show us His will today?

DAY 4 *Ezra 2:64-68.*
a) How do you think the people would feel as they viewed the devastation of their holy city?

b) What should be our attitude when we face some gigantic task?

QUESTIONS (contd.)

DAY 5   *Ezra 2:68, 69.*
a) These people were not only willing to give their service into building the temple, but they also gave their money. Discuss the following verses: Luke 6:35, 2 Corinthians 9:8; Philippians 4:16-19; Proverbs 11:24, 25. What should be the motive of our giving?

b) Can you think of other instances of sacrificial giving in the Bible?

DAY 6   *Exodus 36:4-7; Mark 12:42; Luke 10:33-35; John 12:1-8; etc.*
What can we give to God and to needy people apart from money?

DAY 7   *Ezra 2:70.*
a) The people returned to their ancestral homes in various towns. What would they find after 70 years, and what would they do.

b) What qualities were required to face the problems that lay ahead?

NOTES

THE PREPARATION

Can we imagine the joy of anticipation as the people, including whole families, planned to leave Babylon to see, for the first time, their 'homeland'? Only the aged among them would have had first hand knowledge of Jerusalem, since almost seventy years had passed during their captivity in Babylon. Nevertheless to Jewish people Jerusalem was always 'home', and the temple at Jerusalem the centre of their worship of Jehovah.

Yes, they had (and still have) their local synagogues, but Jerusalem and the temple represented in a special way the presence of God with His people. Notice how Daniel used to pray three times a day facing Jerusalem (Dan. 6:10). To him Jerusalem would always be 'home'.

LIST OF TRAVELLERS

Maybe we can skim over verses 3 to 63, which would mean more to the Jews than to us. Can you imagine a boy a century later proudly affirming, 'See, my great, great grandfather was one of those who left the comforts of Babylon to build our beautiful temple'? Genealogies meant much to Jewish people who could recite their ancestry right back to Abraham.

A list of eleven leaders is given, with Zerubbabel of King David's line as governor, and Joshua (Jeshua in some versions) as High priest, heading the list. (The Nehemiah mentioned is not the man who later built the walls of Jerusalem). Next comes a list of people grouped according to their ancestral towns. Then priests, Levites, singers, temple gate keepers, temple servants and the descendants of the servants of King Solomon. It was quite a formidable company of 42,360 Jewish people, besides 7,337 servants (my! times have changed since Nebuchadnezzar's era). Even horses, mules and donkeys were numbered. The Jews have always been noted for their efficiency, and this businesslike accounting is typical.

THE JOURNEY AND ARRIVAL

The historian tells us nothing of the journey, which today could be accomplished by plane in a couple of hours. But in those days it would require four strenuous months. Imagine the planning in food and water, cooking vessels and clothing to meet their needs through that terrible desert land. But they were to see their holy land. That knowledge would spur them on.

Nothing is mentioned of their horror in eventually arriving at Jerusalem to find a derelict city of broken walls, a temple site full of great stones, and a city in ruins. But these brave people had come to raise a temple out of the rubble, and they knew their God would be with them to enable them to accomplish this task.

A verse to remember:
'But seek first his kingdom and his righteousness, and all these things will be given to you as well' (Matt. 6:33, NIV).

STUDY 3
PROGRESS UNDERWAY

QUESTIONS

DAY 1 *Ezra 3:1; Psalm 133:1-3; Ephesians 4:3.*
a) What does God say about unity?

b) How does this apply to our church situations?

DAY 2 *Ezra 3:2; 1 Corinthians 11:23; 12:1; 14:40; John 16:13.*
a) How did they know how to observe the festival? Leviticus 23:33-36.

b) And how do we know how to conduct our worship?

DAY 3 *Ezra 3:3-6; 1 John 4:18; 2 Timothy 1:7; Psalm 46:1,2; Proverbs 29:25.*
a) What negative emotion did they have to overcome?

b) How can we overcome this?

DAY 4 *Ezra 3:7.*
a) Did the people give from their abundance or sacrificially?

b) With what motives should we give our gifts? 2 Corinthians 9:7.

QUESTIONS (contd.)

DAY 5 *Ezra 3:7-9.*
a) How did King Cyrus help them besides money?

b) Without mechanized help, many of the 42,000 people would have been involved as overseers, masons, carpenters and labourers. How can this kind of co-operation build up our churches today?

DAY 6 *Ezra 3:10-13.*
a) We see emotion expressed by these Jewish people on completion of the foundation. Why are some people afraid of emotion today?

b) What do we, as Christians, have to be excited about?

DAY 7 *Ezra 3:12.*
a) Why were some of the old people so upset?

b) Give examples of how negative criticism can hinder a work?

NOTES

THE FEAST OF TABERNACLES

Now we see Joshua the High Priest taking the lead. As yet the work on the temple had not begun, since the people were still settling into their homes. So in the seventh month the call goes out for all the people to assemble on the temple site to observe the Feast of Tabernacles. This annual festival had special significance for these people so recently arrived after their desert journey. It was a reminder of the long journey their ancestors had taken from Egypt to the promised land, during which time they had lived in tents or booths.

Although there was yet no temple, the altar was built which was the centre of their worship and the means of approaching God through sacrifice. We can imagine the joy of the people as they spent the first week in worship, sacrifice, prayer and in singing psalms of praise. They knew that before long they were going to be able to worship God in their own temple which they would build with their own hands.

THE COMPLETION OF THE FOUNDATION

And now the real work on the temple is about to commence. Again out of their poverty the people bring their offerings of money. Much planning was necessary to bring great cedar logs by raft from Tyre and Sidon, then overland to the temple site in Jerusalem.

The Levites (assistants to the priests) supervised the work of the builders. So eventually the foundation of the temple was completed, and celebrations were the order of the day. We can visualize the priests in their colourful vestments, and the Levites with their instruments, leading the people in singing and shouts of praise and thanksgiving to God. What joy!

And yet, wonder of wonders, the older people were weeping aloud. The temple of King Solomon had been one of the wonders of the world, and they could see, even at this stage of the building, that this temple would be nothing in comparison. The prophet Zechariah, writing in encouragement at this stage, asks, 'Who despises the day of small things?' (Zech. 4:10). Let us beware of comparisons. Where people love God and seek His face, He can be just as present in a humble hall as in a mighty cathedral.

A verse to remember:
'The joy of the Lord is your strength' (Neh. 8:10).

STUDY 4

SATAN'S OPPOSITION

QUESTIONS

DAY 1   *Ezra 4:1-6, Esther 1:1; 2:17.*
After King Cyrus, King Ahasuerus (Xerxes) became king of the Persian empire. Which famous Jewess became his queen?

DAY 2   *Ezra 4:7-10.*
a) Notice the list of officials banded together to make accusations against the Jews. What does that teach us about Satan's methods?

b) Compare the priests' methods in accusing Jesus (Matt. 27:20-22).

DAY 3   *Ezra 4:12; Psalm 122:7; 2 Kings 25:10, 11.*
a) Why was it important for the Jews to build walls around their city?

b) Why did the building of the walls worry the enemy? (Zech. 2:5).

c) What are some walls that we can build around ourselves for our protection against our spiritual enemies? (Isa. 60:18; Prov. 25:28).

QUESTIONS (contd.)

DAY 4 *Ezra 4:13.*

a) Why did they fear that if the walls were built the Jewish people would refuse to pay taxes to the king?

b) At what stage had Jerusalem been a resistant city? (Jer. 38:17-23).

DAY 5 *Ezra 4:11-16.*

a) Do you think the enemies of the Jews were really concerned that the king might lose revenue?

b) What was their motive in writing to the king?

DAY 6 *Ezra 4:17-23.*

a) How do you think the Jews reacted to this letter?

b) What should our attitude be to Jewish people?

DAY 7 *Ezra 4:23.*

a) What positive attitude do you think might have kept their faith alive during the days ahead?

b) How can God use the opposition of Satan for our good?

THE CHRONOLOGY OF THIS SECTION

Why, we wonder, was this section included in this part of the book? You see, it refers to what happened later in the days of Artaxerxes (also called Xerxes or Ahasuerus), when the temple was already completed. Perhaps, while on the subject of persecution, Ezra decided to record this incident. Or maybe some later copyist mistakenly included it at this stage of the story. Whatever happened it is still accurate history, though not in chronological order. So we will look at it here, just as it appears in our Bibles.

THE WRITERS OF THE LETTER TO ARTAXERXES

The letter was written by an imposing list of Persian officials who were over the whole province called BEYOND THE RIVER, which included all the territory from the Euphrates (border of Iraq) to Judea and beyond. These rulers were opposed to the Jewish leaders because of their worship of Jehovah and determined to get royal approval for their plans to stop the building of the temple.

CONTENTS OF THE LETTERS

Notice how subtly they put their case to the king. After pointing out that the Jews had always been a rebellious nation, they appealed to the pride and ambition of the king. If the wall were built the Jews would rebel and refuse to pay taxes. Then:

> The king would suffer financially,
> He would be dishonoured, and
> He would lose part of his empire.

They requested that a search be made in the royal records to verify those facts and appropriate action be taken.

THE KING'S REPLY

A search was made, and no doubt the king read of how the kings of Judah had held out against the invading armies. Order was given to stop the further building of the city and its walls.

RESULT

The enemies of the Jews wasted no time in forcing the cessation of the work. This part of the history seems to finish with verse 23, and verse 24 is a continuation of the previous story, which we will look at in our next lesson.

EZRA • STUDY 4 • SATAN'S OPPOSITION

LESSONS TO LEARN

The main lesson we can learn from this story is surely this: that problems we face in our lives do not necessarily mean that we are out of the will of God. On the contrary, when we are seeking to please God, Satan will seek to use someone to oppose us. In fact, Paul, in reminding Timothy of his own persecutions, asserted, 'indeed all who desire to live a godly life in Christ Jesus shall be persecuted', a fact that our fellow Christians in many countries are experiencing today. Opposition in our Christian lives should not be a cause for discouragement, but a call for FAITH, COURAGE and PERSEVERANCE.

A verse to remember:
> 'May the God of hope fill you with all joy and peace as you trust in him, so that you may overflow with hope, through the power of the Holy Spirit' (Rom. 15:13, NIV).

STUDY 5

OPPOSITION AND RENEWAL

QUESTIONS

DAY 1 *Ezra 4:1-5, 24; 2 Corinthians 6:14.*
a) In spiritual work, should we enlist worldly people to help us? If not, why not?

b) What evidence do we have that the people in Ezra's day were not genuine?

DAY 2 *Ezra 5:1; 1 Corinthians 14:3.*
Why is prophecy given?

DAY 3 *Ezra 5:2.*
a) Why had the people lost interest in continuing the work? (Ezra 4:4, 5).

b) What encouraged Zerubbabel and Joshua to recommence the building?

DAY 4 *Haggai 1.*
a) To whom did Haggai address God's message?

b) What excuse were the people giving for delaying the building of the temple?

c) Did the people obey God's word given through Haggai?

QUESTIONS (contd.)

DAY 5 *Haggai 2.*

a) What are some of the promises God gave them concerning the building of the temple? (vv. 4, 5, 7, 19).

b) The church of today is likened to a temple (Heb. 3:6; I Pet. 2:4,5; Eph. 2:19-22). Can you apply some of these promises to us today?

c) How can we, under the Master Builder, be part of the building of this temple today? (Matt. 16:18).

DAY 6 *Zechariah 3.*

a) Verse 1. What is one of Satan's lines of attack?

b) What should you do when negative thoughts come into your mind concerning yourself or someone else?

c) What are some 'beautiful garments' God speaks to us about in the Bible? (Isa. 61:3, 10; Rev. 19:8; Eph. 6:11; Rom. 13:14).

DAY 7 *Zechariah 4.*

a) What did Zechariah's vision teach Zerubbabel about how he was to accomplish the big task ahead?

b) What encouraging promises did God give to him?

c) As well as encouraging God's people, what else did God's prophets do? (Ezra 5:2). Apply this.

OPPOSITION FROM THE LOCAL PEOPLE

After the excitement of the recent celebrations, events took a new turn. Whenever there is success we can be sure that Satan will raise up opposition. This came in rather a subtle form. Some of the local people, later called Samaritans, people of mixed race, came to Zerubbabel with an offer to help in the building. How easy it would have been to welcome such help, but Zerubbabel was a man of discernment. He recognized their insincerity, and in no uncertain tones refused their help. Their subsequent opposition proved that his decision was right, for they immediately showed their true colours. Jesus told his disciples to be wise as serpents and harmless as doves. How we need to trust God for that spirit of discernment to know when people are genuine. They could do little officially to stop the workers, since the kings Cyrus and Darius had given permission for the building to go ahead. Nevertheless their constant harassment brought about such discouragement that the builders lost interest, and the building of the temple ceased for some years, each man preferring to get involved in his own interests.

RENEWAL UNDER HAGGAI AND ZECHARIAH

It seemed that it was not only the common people who had gone back to their homes and fields, but their two leaders Zerubbabel and Joshua had also become discouraged. God knew that they needed men of faith and vision to set their hearts alight with that spiritual spark again. This encouragement came through two godly prophets. Perhaps one of the most important ministries in the church today is that of encourager. There are plenty of critics around, but God is calling us to encourage one another.

HAGGAI ...

... explains to the people that the poor economic state of the Province and the failure of crops was due to the fact that the people were more concerned with their own interests than in fulfilling the job for which they had returned to Jerusalem. Three times he repeats the phrase 'Take courage', and gives the promise 'I am with you.... My Spirit abides among you.... I will fill this house with splendour'. No wonder his exhortation was successful and the people gladly resumed their task.

ZECHARIAH ...

... has a different message, given to him by God about the same time. He saw two visions. In the one recorded in Zechariah 3 he sees JOSHUA the High Priest, with Satan standing accusing him. Joshua is arrayed in filthy garments, but the angel of the Lord commands that the filthy garments be removed, and he be clothed with clean rich garments fit for God's high priest.

In chapter 4 we read of God's message to ZERUBBABEL. Zechariah sees a vision of a golden lampstand fed from oil flowing from two olive trees (oil always stands for the Holy Spirit in scripture). And God gives him this message for Zerubbabel: ''Not by might nor by power, but by my Spirit,' says the Lord.... The hands of Zerubbabel have laid the foundation of this temple; his hands will also complete it.'

With two such godly men encouraging God's chosen leaders, it was not long before the work recommenced. God's two prophets not only encouraged the leaders and the nation, but they got alongside the builders and helped them in the work. Let's determine, with God's help, that we too will encourage God's people, and be available to help in any practical way we can.

A verse to remember.
'Let us encourage one another – and all the more as you see the Day approaching' (Heb. 10:25, NIV).

STUDY 6

QUESTIONS

DAY 1 *Ezra 5:3-5.*
a) Why did Tattenai question the Jews about the building of the temple?

b) What does the fact that Tattenai did not stop the building during that time indicate?

DAY 2 *Ezra 5:6-11.*
a) In his letter to the king how does he describe the Jewish God?

b) How do the Jewish leaders describe their God?

c) How did Jesus teach us to describe God? (Matt. 6:4, 6, 8, 9, 32).

DAY 3 *Ezra 5:12-17.*
a) What reason do they give for having been taken captive?

b) Did Tattenai try to influence Darius's decision?

DAY 4 *Ezra 6:1-5.*
a) What did Cyrus's original decree say?

QUESTIONS (contd.)

b) How do we see Ephesians 3:20 happening here? Can we claim this too?

DAY 5 *Ezra 6:6-12.*
a) How do we see that King Darius, like King Cyrus, had some degree of faith in the God of Israel? (v. 10)

b) How do we see in these Persian kings a very different attitude from that in the former Babylonian kings?

DAY 6 *Ezra 6:13, 14.*
a) To what did the Jewish people attribute their new found freedom?

b) How does this reinforce the value God places on the ministry of encouragement?

DAY 7 *Ezra 6:15.*
a) They had received permission from King Cyrus to return and rebuild the temple in 536 BC, and they completed it in 515 BC. How long, with stops and starts, had it taken to complete the work?

b) What qualities do we need to enable us to continue living for the Lord?

NOTES

THE LETTER TO THE KING AND HIS REPLY

We see now how wonderfully God answered the prayers of Haggai and Zechariah, and how perfectly He fulfilled the promises he had made through them.

THE LETTER TO KING DARIUS

Although Zerubbabel had been made governor of the province of Judea, Tattenai was governor of the whole region of BEYOND THE EUPHRATES. Therefore he was responsible to Darius King of Persia for all that went on in his area. Hence the letter to the king.

We see a new gracious attitude in the Jewish leaders, as they supplied the facts to Tattenai. After all, Zerubbabel had received a new empowering of the Holy Spirit, and Joshua the High Priest had also been cleansed from his sin of unbelief, fear and apathy and the old zeal was back again. Consequently God was able to work on their behalf, and Tattenai wrote a clear unbiased letter to the king, concerning their work. Zerubbabel told Tattenai of their slavery under Nebuchadnezzar, admitting that it was because of their sin and rebellion. He told of King Cyrus's decree, allowing them to return with the temple treasures to rebuild the temple in Jerusalem. All this was written down and request made that the king authorize a search to verify the facts. The letter was 'posted' by camel mail.

THE REPLY FROM KING DARIUS

Oh, what joy when eventually the reply arrived. Much more than they had ever hoped for! Not only were they permitted to continue with the work in hand, but orders were given that the cost was to be met from the royal revenue. The death sentence was to be carried out on anyone who opposed them. Yes, and this heathen king even prayed for destruction on any king who attempted to destroy the temple they were building.

THE RESULT

The letter to the king had been sent in the second year of Darius's reign, and with God's help and the co-operation of the local authorities, the temple was completed in the sixth year of his reign. Four busy and joyous years of building! As they looked at the completed building, the people were ecstatic. It may not have quite rivalled the magnificent temple King Solomon had built, with the walls, ceilings and floors paved with pure gold. Nevertheless it was a building these Jewish people could be proud of, a building which, by the grace of God and the encouragement of God's prophets, they had built with their own hands. And they knew God was pleased with them.

A verse to remember:
> 'Now to him who is able to do immeasurably more than all we ask or imagine, according to his power that is at work within us, to him be glory...' (Eph. 3:20, 21, NIV).

STUDY 7

TWO GREAT CELEBRATIONS

QUESTIONS

DAY 1 *Ezra 6:16.*
What does the word 'dedication' imply?

DAY 2 *1 Peter 2:5, 9; Revelation 1:6; 5:10; Romans 12:1; Hebrews 13:15, 16; Revelation 8:3, 4.*
a) Who does the New Testament say are God's priests today?

b) What offering can we as priests bring to God?

DAY 3 *Ezra 6:17; Galatians 6:10; 2 Corinthians 5:18, 19.*
a) The priests offered 12 goats as a sin offering for the 12 tribes, although the 10 northern tribes were still in slavery in Assyria. What was their attitude to their backslidden brethren?

b) What should our attitude be to those who have not received Jesus?

DAY 4 *Ezra 6:16-18.*
As Christians, every aspect of life is sacred (1 Cor. 10:31). How can we eat food to the glory of God?

QUESTIONS (contd.)

DAY 5 *Ezra 6:19-21; I Corinthians 11:28, 29.*
a) Who was allowed to eat this Passover?

b) What is the Christian celebration in which this occasion finds its fulfilment? Who can partake of this?

DAY 6 *Ezra 6:22.*
a) When all the people were able to partake with pure hearts, what emotion followed? Why was this?

b) What is the secret of being a joyful Christian?

DAY 7 *Ezra 6:22; Proverbs 16:7.*
a) What was the reason for the king being so helpful to them?

b) How had he gone beyond just giving them permission to continue with the building?

NOTES

THE DEDICATION OF THE TEMPLE

The beautiful building stood out against the sky on the site where 70 years earlier the magnificent temple of Solomon had been looted and destroyed by Nebuchadnezzar's army. It was 20 years since the Jewish remnant had celebrated the laying of the foundation of their new temple. Now their joy knew no bounds as they celebrated the completion of their task.

We can picture the scene, as the priests lay aside their work clothes for their priestly garments. The orchestra and choir are in place, and psalms of David are sung with fervour. The people have brought many offerings which have been slaughtered, the fat and innards removed and burned on the altar, and the meat eaten in joyful celebration by all the people. Then, remembering their brethren from the 10 northern tribes still in captivity in Assyria, and their Jewish friends in Babylon, they offered 12 male goats as a sin offering. These sin offerings pointed forward to the time when Jesus the spotless Lamb of God would offer himself for the sin of all mankind.

THE PASSOVER CELEBRATION

One month later there was another important occasion. It had been many years since the Feast of Passover had been celebrated, and for most of the people this would have been a new experience. It would have had special significance for a people so recently returned from captivity, as they remembered the time, nearly 1,000 years earlier, when God had delivered their ancestors from captivity in Egypt to bring them to their promised land. As at that first Passover so now, each family would select a lamb without blemish, keep it for four days, then slaughter, cook and eat it with thanksgiving. This celebration also looked forward to the day, nearly 500 years later, when Jesus would sacrifice himself on Passover day to be the Redeemer of all of us.

The Feast of Unleavened Bread that followed recalled the exodus when their ancestors left Egypt in haste with no time to mix yeast with their dough. The same sort of non-yeast wholemeal bread is eaten in many eastern countries today as round 'pancakes'.

What a lovely verse is verse 22! 'For seven days they celebrated with joy the Feast of Unleavened bread, because THE LORD HAD FILLED THEM WITH JOY.' What a contrast from the dispirited bunch of impoverished, disillusioned people who had left off the work for 15 long years some time earlier. Only the Lord could have brought about this transformation.

A verse to remember:
> 'Do you not know that your body is a temple of the Holy Spirit, who is in you, whom you have received from God' (1 Cor. 6:19, NIV).

STUDY 8

ENTER EZRA

QUESTIONS

DAY 1 *Ezra 7:1-6.*
a) How is Ezra described in verse 6?

b) How can we become skilled in God's Word?

DAY 2 *Ezra 7:6; Proverbs 21:1.*
a) To whom does Ezra credit the change in the king's attitude?

b) How can we influence our government towards righteousness?

DAY 3 *Ezra 7:7-10.*
a) What was Ezra's threefold attitude to the Word of God?

b) You are doing the first part right now. What are the remaining two aspects that you should carry out, and how?

DAY 4 *Ezra 7:11-23.*
a) What gifts can we give to God and His people?

b) How do we sense that the king had absolute trust in Ezra's honesty?

QUESTIONS (contd.)

DAY 5 *Ezra 7:19-23; John 14:23; Galatians 5:13.*
a) What was one reason for the king's generosity?

b) With what motive should we serve Him and others?

DAY 6 *Ezra 7:24-26; James 1:5, 6.*
a) What responsibility did the king give Ezra?

b) What statement shows that even the king realized that Ezra's wisdom was not mere human wisdom?

c) If we lack wisdom in any situation, what should we do?

DAY 7 *Ezra 7:27-28; Ephesians 5:20.*
For what does Ezra praise and bless God here? And the result?

NOTES

ENTER EZRA

As we explained in the introduction, although Ezra is the author of the book called by his name, he does not appear on the scene until about 60 years after the dedication of the temple. By now Zerubbabel and Joshua would have passed on, and little is known of what has happened in Judea during the intervening years. The history we have looked at in chapters 1 to 5 would later have been recorded by Ezra with the help of records kept during those years, since the Jewish people always kept records of all the events of their history. There would also be some who had been young at the time of the dedication of the temple who would have been able to give Ezra a firsthand account of that great occasion.

THE DESCRIPTION OF EZRA

Ezra appears to be a remarkable man. He was apparently an officer in the government of Artaxerxes king of Persia, perhaps with a position such as 'ministry of Jewish affairs'! He was a direct descendant of Aaron the first High Priest of Israel, and is described as a 'scribe skilled in the law of Moses' (v. 6). And verse 10 tells us 'Ezra had set his heart to STUDY the law and to DO it and to TEACH his statutes and ordinances in Israel.'

PURPOSE OF HIS JOURNEY

Although we know little of what had happened in Israel after the completion of the temple, it would appear that, with the passing on of their Jewish leaders, the Jewish people were lacking in competent teachers, and therefore there was unrest. The king of Persia did his best to keep all parts of his vast empire happy and at peace, and therefore he chose out the best Jewish teacher to go to the land of Judea to set things in order.

Zerubbabel and Joshua, Haggai and Zechariah, had done the spade work, the people had been moulded into a nation on their own soil again, and the temple worship had been re-established. Now God brings to Jerusalem another skilled man to establish the work they had so ably commenced.

THE KING'S LETTER

The king seems to be familiar with the required worship of the Lord. Perhaps Ezra has instructed him. And so a letter is written supplying materials to beautify the temple, and allowing a further contingent of people to accompany Ezra to their land. The king realizes that it is to his advantage to be generous to the Jewish people in their worship. He also empowers Ezra to appoint magistrates, not only over Judea but over the laws of God they were to be taught. Thus the great king of the Persian empire recognizes that knowledge of the laws of the God of Israel will bring peace and prosperity to this section of his dominion. Pray that the rulers of our nation might realize this today.

A verse to remember:
    '...set an example to the believers in speech, in life, in love, in faith and in purity' (1 Tim. 4:12).

STUDY 9

EZRA'S JOURNEY

QUESTIONS

DAY 1   *Ezra 8:1, 15-20.*
a) What kind of people were missing in this company? What does this teach us about the place each of us has to play in the service of God?

b) Read 1 Corinthians 12:14-27 and comment on the lessons taught here.

DAY 2   *Ezra 8:21 (Matthew 4:1, 2; Luke 2:37-38; Acts 13:1-3).*
a) Ezra proclaimed a fast. What was the reason given?

b) For what reasons did the people in the N.T. references fast?

DAY 3   *Ezra 8:22-30.*
a) Why did Ezra not ask the king for a company of soldiers to protect them?

b) Share any personal experiences of God's protection.

DAY 4   *1 John 2:16; Galatians 5:19-21; 1 Peter 5:8, 9.*
Ezra wanted God's protection against natural enemies, brigands, etc. Discuss the spiritual enemies we need God's protection from.

QUESTIONS (contd.)

DAY 5 *Ezra 8:31, 32; Mark 6:31.*
a) Jesus once took his disciples aside for a time of rest. Does God want us to have times of relaxation?

b) Discuss Matthew 11:28-30.

DAY 6 *Ezra 8:33, 34; Matthew 25:14-30; Luke 16:10.*
a) What lessons can we learn in the way the treasures were weighed and handed across to the priests in Jerusalem?

b) Look at the parable of the talents, and apply this to yourselves.

DAY 7 *Ezra 8:35, 36.*
a) How did the returned exiles show their gratitude to God for their safe arrival?

b) In what further way did God show his favour to his people? (v. 36).

NOTES

EZRA'S JOURNEY

What a great procession of people volunteered to accompany Ezra to the land of their fathers! They had felt God's call to leave the familiar for the unfamiliar, the comfort of life in Persia for a life of possible discomfort and poverty in Israel. They were facing the unknown. Four months of journey across an unknown desert would be a tremendous challenge for the men, but more so for their wives and children. There were probably about 3,000 making the journey.

THE PREPARATION FOR THE JOURNEY

As well as packing and preparation of food for such a long journey with no supermarkets or even corner stores on the way, there was also the spiritual preparation. They were not trained in war, and they knew they would be helpless against the bands of bandits along the way. There were also other dangers to meet in the deserts of Iraq – scorching heat by day and sub zero temperatures by night. There would be no help if sickness struck. They had to be men and women of FAITH, COURAGE and PERSEVERANCE.

Ezra, as the one in charge of so large a party felt responsible. As he was in the king's favour he could have asked for a band of soldiers to protect them, but he had already told the king about their mighty God who protects His people. So now he is determined to put his whole trust in God.

So there, camped for 3 days by the Ahava Canal, the whole company spent time in prayer and fasting. Is this applicable to us today? We find that fasting was practised in the New Testament as well as in the Old Testament. Where fasting is carried out with prayer, especially where there is a special need or challenge, prayer becomes more effective.

THE JOURNEY

Ezra does not give us any details as to how they fared during that long journey. He made light of the difficulties and hardships of the way. But his thrice repeated comment was 'the hand of our God was on us'. And so, protected from enemies and the dangers of the road, the journey was completed. Three days of rest were taken, and then the people settled into their new life. We too are on a journey. It started when we were conceived in our mothers' wombs, and it continues till we reach our promised land, where Jesus is even now making preparations for us. There are difficulties and dangers on the road. (Have you read *Pilgrim's Progress*?) There are enemies who would try to trip us up. But let us remember like Ezra that we have a mighty God whose powerful and loving hand is guiding us each step of the way. Let us put our whole confidence in him.

A verse to remember:

'Trust in the Lord with all your heart and lean not on your own understanding. In all your ways acknowledge him, and he will direct your paths' (Prov. 3:5, 6).

STUDY 10

RENEWAL UNDER EZRA

QUESTIONS

DAY 1   *Ezra 9:1, 2; 2 Corinthians 6:14, 15.*
a) Why did God make a law prohibiting intermarriage with the nations around them?

b) Why is it not right for a Christian to marry a good living unbeliever?

DAY 2   *Ezra 9:3.*
Why was Ezra so appalled at the news?

DAY 3   *Ezra 9:5-15; Daniel 9:4-19.*
Look at Ezra's prayer, and compare it with Daniel's which had been prayed years before in Babylon. What can we learn from these two prayers about praying for our nation?

DAY 4   a) Look at 2 Chronicles 7:14, and write down the steps needed in praying for our nation.

b) Did Ezra and Daniel observe each of these steps, and did God answer their prayer?

QUESTIONS (contd.)

DAY 5 *Ezra 10:1-6.*
a) How was Ezra's prayer answered?

b) How does God use prayer to change people's attitudes?

DAY 6 *Ezra 10:7-17.*
a) How did Ezra combine action with his faith?

b) How did the people show respect to the authority God had given to Ezra?

c) And how should we show respect to those whom God has placed in leadership over us? (Titus 3:1; Heb. 13:17).

DAY 7 *Nehemiah 8:1-18.*
a) When Ezra read the book of the law from daybreak to noon, what was the attitude of the people?

b) As well as reading the Word, what else did he do?

c) Share some lesson from the book of Ezra that has been a blessing.

CONCLUSION

We come to our last study in the book of Ezra. On the surface these two chapters seem to place a damper on all the exciting things we have read in the first eight chapters. Yet perhaps we see in these two chapters as in no other part of the book a picture of God's standard of holiness. We see too that even when we fall, there is a way back to enjoy God's forgiveness and restoration.

ISRAEL'S FAILURE

Where is the revival that took place earlier under the godly leadership of Zerubbabel and Joshua, Haggai and Zechariah? Once again God's standards have been flouted, perhaps because of lack of clear teaching of God's law. God had clearly warned the nation through Moses not to intermarry with the nations around them 'for they will turn your sons away from me to serve other gods'. God is not racist, neither should we be.

However, God knew that the people of the nations around them had many abominable practices, including sex perversions and child sacrifices, as part of their demonic worship, and it is thought that they were also heavily infected with venereal disease. God loved these people and he wanted the Jewish people to be a light to the nations. But he knew that intermarriage was not the way to accomplish this. There are many instances in the Jewish history to show that when this took place God's people adopted the evil practices of their partners who did not share their faith. It is the same today, for 'What fellowship has light with darkness?' asked Paul.

EZRA'S ATTITUDE

It is clear that when Ezra was told about the extent of this sin he considered it no light matter. We may think he overreacted as we see him tearing his garment, pulling out his hair and refusing to eat – a picture of utter devastation. Yet he loved his nation greatly and dreaded that they would again fall into a state of backsliding and God's blessing be removed. His concern was for God's honour and that God's holiness be vindicated. What could he do? His only resource was prayer.

EZRA'S PRAYER

What a lesson in intercession there is for us in Ezra's prayer. You notice the pronoun 'we' is used, not 'they'. Ezra totally identifies himself with the sin of his nation – 'our sin', 'our guilt', 'we have disobeyed your commands', 'What has happened to us is the result of our evil deeds and our great guilt'. We have here a pattern for praying for ourselves and for our nation:

genuine sorrow
>honest confession
>>declaration of God's righteousness
>>>recognition that God's punishment is justified, yet
>>>>throwing themselves on God's mercy.

PUTTING THINGS RIGHT

Admission of fault was not enough, matters must be rectified. God abundantly answered Ezra's prayer by causing the full co-operation of the people who had sinned. The steps Ezra took may seem harsh by today's standards. The non-Israelite wives and their children must be sent away. But with the exception of very few, the whole nation was so convicted of their sin that all co-operated, so that they might again experience the blessing of God. And on this note the book of Ezra ends. Yet we have a final glimpse of Ezra in the book of Nehemiah, the man God raised up to build the walls of Jerusalem. In Nehemiah chapter 8 we see Ezra standing on a raised platform reading from the scrolls the laws of Moses, and explaining their meaning to the hundreds of men, women and children who were standing in the city square. This continued for the full week of the Festival of Tabernacles, the time being divided between reading the Word, confession and worshipping the Lord. How blessed we are to have Bibles of our own, a privilege that people of that day could hardly have dreamt of.

The conclusion of Ezra's teaching was 'Go and enjoy good food and sweet drinks, and send some to those for whom nothing is prepared. This day is sacred to the Lord. Do not grieve, for THE JOY OF THE LORD IS YOUR STRENGTH.'

A verse to remember:
>'If we confess our sins He is faithful and just to forgive us our sins, and cleanse us from all unrighteousness' (I John 1:9).

ANSWER GUIDE

The following pages contain an Answer Guide. It is recommended that answers to the questions be attempted before turning to this guide. It is only a guide and the answers given should not be treated as exhaustive.

GUIDE TO STUDY 1

DAY 1 a) Prophecies concerning Jesus' second coming.
b) Since the prophecies recorded in the Old Testament have been so accurately fulfilled, we can know that God who cannot lie will fulfil all prophecies.

DAY 2 Although God does not force anyone to do His will, our prayers will tend to soften their hearts and cause Satan's influence over them to be diminished, so that they can be drawn towards God and His will.

DAY 3 a) To the Lord, the God of heaven, not to his heathen idols.
b) By the Bible, by putting His desires into our hearts as we seek His will, by godly advice from others, especially from those in authority in the church. Very occasionally by dreams or visions.

DAY 4 a) The heads of the families, the priests and the Levites, followed by the ordinary people whose hearts God had moved.
b) The Holy Spirit, through the leaders God has placed over us, supported by the congregation. Members should discuss new visions God has given them with the church leadership for their approval and co-operation.

DAY 5 Because they now owned possessions of their own.

DAY 6 a) By giving material help.
b) It is the responsibility of Christian people. Each church should support those they set aside for full time Christian work.

DAY 7 a) He was honest, generous and businesslike.
b) Definitely. They must be accountable for all monies entrusted to them

GUIDE TO STUDY 2

DAY 1   Mainly desert.

DAY 2   a) Priests, Levites, singers, gatekeepers, temple servants.
b) Family relationships harmonious. Character above reproach. Know the Bible and be able to impart that knowledge. A sense of God's call.

DAY 3   God guides through the Bible, through our inner conviction after earnest prayer, confirmation through mature Christians, a settled inner peace.

DAY 4   a) They would hardly have been prepared to see such devastation. Yet they knew that God had brought them safely there and He would enable them to accomplish the job they had come to do.
b) Recognize the difficulties, but know that God is bigger than the difficulties, and He will enable.

DAY 5   a) The motive for our giving should not be for reward, but be prompted by our love for God and for needy people. The joy of seeing needs met is sufficient reward.
b) As in references.

DAY 6   We can give love, time, use of car and other possessions, food, encouragement, prayer, manual labour, items we can make by sewing, knitting, baking, carpentry.

DAY 7   a) Their homes ruined, fields a jungle. Make homes liveable, and so devote their energy to building the temple.
b) Faith, courage and perseverance.

GUIDE TO STUDY 3

DAY 1   a) Unity is likened to oil and dew, both pictures of the Holy Spirit, who is the source of true unity. Note, it comes down, a picture of its heavenly origin.
b) He will bring unity if we co-operate with Him. Where there is love and unity among the church leaders unity will naturally flow among the members. Nothing destroys a fellowship like disunity.

DAY 2   a) God had instructed them through Moses.
b) We have the Word of God and the Spirit of God to direct us.

DAY 3   a) Fear.
b) We must realize that fear is not of God, and, that as we trust in His love and know that He is with us, we can overcome it.

DAY 4   a) They gave sacrificially.
b) We should give cheerfully, not for any reward, but from the desire to bless others.

DAY 5   a) He gave instructions to the rulers of Tyre and Sidon to supply the needed timber.
b) Everyone has a task to do. Some are in the limelight with specialized ministries, others are 'helps' often doing jobs that seem unimportant, but not to God.

DAY 6   a) Partly our temperament or the way our emotions may have been repressed as children. But we can learn to be spontaneous just as a little child.
b) For all spiritual blessings, as well as the supply of all our material and physical needs.

DAY 7   a) Because they realized this temple would be inferior to the one they had known as children.
b) Unfair criticism, comparing a fellowship unfavourably with another.

GUIDE TO STUDY 4

DAY 1   Queen Esther.

DAY 2   a) He uses a few forceful people to enlist others to oppose God's purposes.
b) The priests persuaded the multitudes to cry out, 'Crucify him'.

DAY 3   a) For its protection against enemies.
b) Because it would make it more difficult for them to oppose the Jews.
c) A fervent trust in God to be our protection. A constant attitude of praise to God for saving us. Exercising self control when tempted.

DAY 4   a) They thought the walls would be a protection against any army the king might send to subdue them.
b) They had resisted the army of Babylon which had conquered all other lands, against God's command through Jeremiah to surrender.

DAY 5   a) No.
b) They hated the Jews and wanted to show off their authority.

DAY 6   a) They knew they were obeying God in building the walls and city, so would have been confused and distressed by the king's reply.
b) Christians should be grateful to the Jews for giving us our Bible and our Saviour. We should show love, and witness to Jewish people about Jesus their Messiah.

DAY 7   a) Faith that God had sent them to do the work and would open the way at the right time. In other words – FAITH, COURAGE and PERSEVERANCE.
b) Many examples of missionaries being refused visas, and consequently God sending them to an area of greater fruitfulness. Young people not getting into their chosen career because God was calling them to something better.

GUIDE TO STUDY 5

DAY 1 a) No, because they would use worldly methods and not rely on the Spirit of God to guide them.
b) They had been recognized as enemies (v. 1), and they reacted to the leaders' refusal by doing all they could to hinder the further building of the temple.

DAY 2 A prophet is defined as 'one who announces the declarations of God'; he is God's mouthpiece to strengthen, comfort and encourage God's people.

DAY 3 a) They were discouraged because of the opposition of the enemies around them.
b) The words of God through the two prophets Haggai and Zechariah.

DAY 4 a) To the two leaders Zerubbabel and Joshua.
b) That it wasn't the time. It could wait till they had attended to their own affairs.
c) Yes.

DAY 5 a) I am with you. My Spirit remains among you. I will fill this house with glory. From this day on I will bless you.
b) Apply these promises to yourself and your church.
c) By bringing people to know Jesus, and by being an encourager to God's people.

DAY 6 a) He accuses God's people to themselves and to others.
b) When they are false and we know that they are from Satan, we should refuse to entertain them knowing that God loves and accepts us (or the other person) in the Lord Jesus Christ.
c) The garments of praise, of salvation, of righteousness, of good deeds, and the whole armour of God to protect us.

DAY 7 a) To rely on the Spirit of God to guide and empower him.
b) The mountains of difficulty would be removed and his hands would complete the work he had started.
c) They prayed for them, encouraged them, and worked alongside the people in the practical work.

GUIDE TO STUDY 6

DAY 1
a) Because he was responsible to the king for whatever happened in his region.
b) That he was not opposed to the Jews, but was making sure that what they were doing had the king's approval.

DAY 2
a) The great God.
b) The God of heaven and earth.
c) Father.

DAY 3
a) They had angered God by their sin and rebellion.
b) No. He gave the king the clear facts and left him to investigate the matter.

DAY 4
a) Here it is recorded that Cyrus gave the exact measurements. Also that the cost was to be met from the royal revenue.
b) God had caused these records to be read, and had provided for His people financially. Yes.

DAY 5
a) He asked them to pray for him and his sons.
b) The Babylonian kings had been cruel tyrants. The Persian kings, by whom God had replaced them, were reasonable, just kings.

DAY 6
a) To the encouragement received through Haggai and Zechariah and to the co-operation of the Persian kings.
b) It was because of the renewal in their hearts through the ministry of God's prophets, that God was able to work on their behalf.

DAY 7
a) Around 21 years.
b) FAITH, COURAGE and PERSEVERANCE.

GUIDE TO STUDY 7

DAY 1   To devote to a sacred purpose.

DAY 2   a) All believers are God's priests.
b) Thanksgiving, praise, prayer, giving.

DAY 3   a) They were concerned that they also should repent and be restored to their own land.
b) We should pray for them, show love and concern, and where possible witness to them about God's love for them.

DAY 4   By being truly thankful for the Lord's provision, and expressing thanks. By enjoying fellowship over food with others. By eating wisely!

DAY 5   a) Priests, Levites, the exiles, and those who had kept true to God.
b) The Lord's Supper (Holy Communion, the Eucharist). If we have confessed and forsaken all sin and received God's forgiveness which Jesus offers through His blood, we are able to partake in a worthy fashion.

DAY 6   a) Joy. The Lord had put joy in their hearts.
b) Living in an attitude of thanksgiving, praise and obedience.

DAY 7   a) It was God's work in his heart.
b) He had helped them with finances, and warned the people of the land against hindering the Jews in their work.

GUIDE TO STUDY 8

DAY 1 a) A scribe or teacher, skilled in the law of Moses which the Lord the God of Israel had given.
b) By reading, studying and meditating on it.

DAY 2 a) To God.
b) By consistent prayer. At times He may lead us to write a letter to our MP, to the local newspaper, or sign a petition. But dependence must be on God to work.

DAY 3 a) To study it, observe or carry it out, and teach it.
b) We can all carry out the lessons we learn from the study. By bringing others along, or by sharing what we learn we can also teach it. There are other opportunities such as teaching Sunday School, etc.

DAY 4 a) Our money, our talents, our time. Also practical helps.
b) He not only gave him valuable gifts to take for the temple, but gave him permission to requisition from the treasurers anything else he should need.

DAY 5 a) The king knew he would not abuse this trust. He knew that Ezra was in such close touch with God and His law that he would know what God required.
b) Love is the only worthy motive.

DAY 6 a) To appoint magistrates who knew God's law, or if they didn't, to teach them.
b) 'According to the wisdom of your God which is in your hand'.
c) To ask for it, believing that God will give it.

DAY 7 He recognizes that it was God who had put the thought into the king's heart to beautify the temple in Jerusalem. It was God who had caused the king and his counsellors to entrust such a great task to him.
He took courage knowing that the hand of his God was upon him.

GUIDE TO STUDY 9

DAY 1 a) Levites and temple servants.
There is a place for all. And our spiritual leaders cannot function effectively without the support of those who seem to be less important.
b) No one can feel he/she has no place to function in Jesus' body. Nor can anyone despise or belittle another, all have a work to do.

DAY 2 a) To humble themselves before God and ask for a safe journey.
b) Jesus fasted 40 days to prepare for his 3 years ministry. Anna served God with prayer and fasting with the hope of seeing the promised Redeemer, and she saw Him. The church at Antioch fasted and prayed, and God called Paul and Barnabas from their midst to serve Him overseas.

DAY 3 a) Because he wanted to prove to the king that they had a great God who would protect them.
b) Personal.

DAY 4 John writes of the lust (desire) of the flesh and the lust of the eyes and the pride of life. Satan works on our own natural desires and emotions to get us to go beyond the bounds that God has set.

DAY 5 a) Yes.
b) We should not live in a state of tension. Jesus, though busy, was always relaxed in spirit, so He invites us to come to Him for inner rest, which we can experience even when busy.

DAY 6 a) It is essential to be scrupulously honest in financial matters, both in personal, church, Mission matters, etc.
b) Some are very talented, others less, but all have talents. God expects us to make use of what we have, and as we use them, God will be able to trust us with more.

DAY 7 a) By offerings of animal sacrifices.
b) By causing the governors of the land to heed the instructions of the king, and give them the assistance they needed.

GUIDE TO STUDY 10

DAY 1 a) Because the Jewish people would follow the evil practices of their partners.
b) Because there would be no spiritual fellowship. Praying and reading God's Word together is a most important side of married life.

DAY 2 Because he wanted God's people to be a holy nation, enjoying God's blessing and being a joy to Him.

DAY 3 We must identify ourselves as part of our nation, and pray for God's mercy, not His justice.

DAY 4 a) Humble ourselves, pray, seek God's face, turn from evil.
b) Yes.

DAY 5 a) The people wept, confessed their sin, and made a promise to God to put away their heathen wives, and they honoured their promise.
b) God's Holy Spirit convicts of sin, so that it becomes easier for the people to do what is right.

DAY 6 a) By ordering the people to assemble in Jerusalem so that the matter could be dealt with.
b) By obeying him and assembling in Jerusalem.
c) By submitting to their leadership, praying for them and encouraging them in their office.

DAY 7 a) They listened attentively.
b) He explained its meaning.

NOTES

OLD TESTAMENT

Triumphs Over Failures: A Study in Judges ISBN 1-85792-888-1 (below left)
Messenger of Love: A Study in Malachi ISBN 1-85792-885-7
The Beginning of Everything: A Study in Genesis 1-11 ISBN 0-90806-728-3
Hypocrisy in Religion: A Study in Amos ISBN 0-90806-706-2
Unshakeable Confidence: A Study in Habakkuk & Joel ISBN 0-90806-751-8
A Saviour is Promised: A Study in Isaiah 1 - 39 ISBN 0-90806-755-0
The Throne and Temple: A Study in 1 & 2 Chronicles ISBN 1-85792-910-1
Our Magnificent God: A Study in Isaiah 40 - 66 ISBN 1-85792-909-8
The Cost of Obedience: A Study in Jeremiah ISBN 0-90806-761-5
Focus on Faith: A Study of 10 Old Testament Characters ISBN 1-85792-890-3

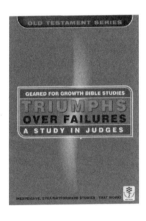
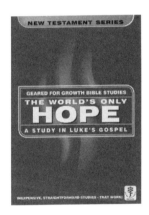

NEW TESTAMENT

The World's Only Hope: A Study in Luke ISBN 1-85792-886-5 (above right)
Walking in Love: A Study in John's Epistles ISBN 1-85792-891-1
Faith that Works: A Study in James ISBN 0-90806-701-1
Made Completely New: A Study in Colossians & Philemon ISBN 0-90806-721-6
Jesus-Christ, Who is He? A Study in John's Gospel ISBN 0-90806-716-X
Entering by Faith: A Study in Hebrews ISBN 1-85792-914-4
Heavenly Living: A Study in Ephesians ISBN 1-85792-911-X
The Early Church: A Study in Acts 1-12 ISBN 0-90806-736-4
The Only Way to be Good: A Study in Romans ISBN 1-85792-950-0
Get Ready: A Study in 1 & 2 Thessalonians ISBN 1-85792-948-9

EZRA

. . . . .

CHARACTERS

Abraham: A Study of Genesis 12-25 ISBN 1-85792-887-3 (below left)
Serving the Lord: A Study of Joshua ISBN 1-85792-889-X
Achieving the Impossible: A Study of Nehemiah ISBN 0-90806-707-0
God plans for Good: A Study of Joseph ISBN 0-90806-700-3
A Man After God's Own Heart: A Study of David ISBN 0-90806-746-1
Grace & Grit: A Study of Ruth & Esther ISBN 1-85792-908-X
Men of Courage: A Study of Elijah & Elisha ISBN 1-85792-913-6
Meek but Mighty: A Study of Moses ISBN 1-85792-951-9

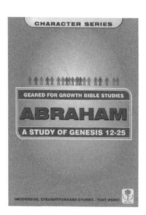 

THEMES

God's Heart, My Heart: World Mission ISBN 1-85792-892-X (above right)
Freedom: You Can Find it! ISBN 0-90806-702-X
Freely Forgiven: A Study in Redemption ISBN 0-90806-720-8
The Problems of Life! Is there an Answer? ISBN 1-85792-907-1
Understanding the Way of Salvation ISBN 0-90082-880-3
Saints in Service: 12 Bible Characters ISBN 1-85792-912-8
Finding Christ in the Old Testament: Pre-existence and Prophecy
ISBN 0-90806-739-9

THE WORD WORLDWIDE

We first heard of WORD WORLDWIDE over 20 years ago when Marie Dinnen, its founder, shared excitedly about the wonderful way ministry to one needy woman had exploded to touch many lives. It was great to see the Word of God being made central in the lives of thousands of men and women, then to witness the life-changing results of them applying the Word to their circumstances. Over the years the vision for WORD WORLDWIDE has not dimmed in the hearts of those who are involved in this ministry. God is still at work through His Word and in today's self-seeking society, the Word is even more relevant to those who desire true meaning and purpose in life. WORD WORLDWIDE is a ministry of WEC International, an interdenominational missionary society, whose sole purpose is to see Christ known, loved and worshipped by all, particularly those who have yet to hear of His wonderful name. This ministry is a vital part of our work and we warmly recommend the WORD WORLDWIDE 'Geared for Growth' Bible studies to you. We know that as you study His Word you will be enriched in your personal walk with Christ. It is our hope that as you are blessed through these studies, you will find opportunities to help others discover a personal relationship with Jesus. As a mission we would encourage you to work with us to make Christ known to the ends of the earth.

Stewart and Jean Moulds – British Directors, **WEC International**.

A full list of over 50 'Geared for Growth' studies can be obtained from:

John and Ann Edwards
5 Louvaine Terrace, Hetton-le-Hole, Tyne & Wear, DH5 9PP
Tel. 0191 5262803 Email: rhysjohn.edwards@virgin.net

Anne Jenkins
2 Windermere Road, Carnforth, Lancs., LA5 9AR
Tel. 01524 734797 Email: anne@jenkins.abelgratis.com

UK Website: www.gearedforgrowth.co.uk

Christian Focus Publications

publishes books for all ages

Our mission statement –

STAYING FAITHFUL

In dependence upon God we seek to help make His infallible word, the Bible, relevant. Our aim is to ensure that the Lord Jesus Christ is presented as the only hope to obtain forgiveness of sin, live a useful life and look forward to heaven with Him.

REACHING OUT

Christ's last command requires us to reach out to our world with His gospel. We seek to help fulfil that by publishing books that point people towards Jesus and help them develop a Christ-like maturity. We aim to equip all levels of readers for life, work, ministry and mission.

Books in our adult range are published in three imprints.

Christian Focus contains popular works including biographies, commentaries, basic doctrine, and Christian living. Our children's books are also published in this imprint.

Mentor focuses on books written at a level suitable for Bible College and seminary students, pastors, and other serious readers; the imprint includes commentaries, doctrinal studies, examination of current issues, and church history.

Christian Heritage contains classic writings from the past.

For details of our titles visit us on our website
www.christianfocus.com

Christian Focus Publications, Ltd
Geanies House, Fearn,
Ross-shire, IV20 ITW, Scotland, United Kingdom
info@christianfocus.com